Get to grips with budgets

How to take the stress out of working with numbers

BLOOMSBURY

A BLOOMSBURY REFERENCE BOOK
Created from the Bloomsbury Business Database
www.ultimatebusinessresource.com

© Bloomsbury Publishing Plc 2005

First published in 2005 by
Bloomsbury Publishing Plc
38 Soho Square
London W1D 3HB

British Library Cataloguing in Publication Data
A CIP record for this book is available from the British Library.

ISBN 0–7475–7734–X

Design by Fiona Pike, Pike Design, Winchester
Typeset by RefineCatch Limited, Bungay, Suffolk
Printed in Italy by Legoprint

All papers used by Bloomsbury Publishing are natural, recyclable products made from wood grown in well-managed forests. The manufacturing processes conform to the environmental regulations of the country of origin.

Contents

Have you got to grips with budgets yet?

Answer the questions and work out your score. Then read the guidance points to find out how you can improve your project management skills.

How do you feel when dealing with numbers?
a) Positive and in control.
b) I do my best and ask for help if I'm not sure.
c) I hope they will look after themselves.

Which of the following do you most closely associate with the word 'budget'?
a) Target and challenge.
b) Stress and inevitability.
c) Constraint and chore.

How well do you cope with financial matters?
a) Fine. I feel quite confident with figures.
b) So-so. I have some experience, but get confused by the terminology.
c) Not very well. I don't know where to start.

When planning a budget, do you factor in a contingency in case things go wrong?
a) Yes. I set funds aside to allow for unforeseen expenses.
b) No. I plan expenditure and income very carefully and don't envisage any problems.
c) No. I don't think it's necessary.

In a company you believe budgeting concerns:
a) Everyone.
b) Just the senior employees.
c) Those working in the finance department.

A 'cash crisis' is:
a) A short-term problem to be solved as soon as possible.
b) A real worry and potential business failure.
c) A nightmare.

Do you check invoices when they come in from suppliers?
a) Yes. Mistakes are easily made but they can mount up.
b) Sometimes.
c) No. I'm sure they're all fine.

What do you do if a customer is late paying you?
a) I ring them up as a first step to see exactly what the problem is.
b) I send them a shirty letter.
c) Not much, really. Most people pay up in the end.

a = 1, b = 2, and c = 3.
Now add up your scores.

- **8–12:** You're already financially aware and have realised the key rule that everyone needs to budget for a 'rainy day'. Chapter **3** offers advice on how to take your budgeting skills up to the next level. Chapters **4–7** will help you be paid on time and get over any cash-flow crises. Chapters **8** and **9** are particularly useful if you run your own business.

- **13–18:** You've got some basic financial knowledge but need a bit of support. Chapter **1** will be useful for you as it explains many key terms without jargon so that you can start to build on your knowledge confidently. If you run your own business or are responsible for budgets in somebody else's, chapters **5** and **6** will help make sure *you* get paid on time and that you can afford to pay others what you owe them!

- **19–24:** Don't panic! You don't have a lot of confidence with numbers, but if you've bought this book, you realise you have to do something about it. Don't assume that because you struggled with maths at school, you'll never be able to get to grips with numbers. Turn to chapters **1** and **2** for confidence-boosting advice on understanding financial terms and creating a basic budget.

Facing up to figures

Numbers just aren't everyone's cup of tea. If you are one of those people, the prospect of having to deal with figures at work may fill you with dread, but don't panic. You're not alone, and with some practice you'll soon feel a lot more comfortable.

Being good (or at least comfortable!) with numbers is a great skill to have, and one that will stand you in great stead if you want to move up your chosen career ladder or start your own business.

Step one: Don't panic!

I I was dreadful at maths when I was at school. Won't it be the same old story now?

No, not necessarily. Lots of people actually gain confidence with numbers as they get older as they feel under less pressure—you're not often put under the spotlight on your own, as you may have been at school. It is hard when you're panicky about something, but the best thing you can do is relax as stress can have an adverse effect on your memory—your mind really does go blank! If you keep calm, you'll make fewer mistakes.

Remember too that when you work with numbers as part of your job, you won't have to get by with just a pen, some paper, and a calculator as you used to. There are lots of easy-to-use software packages, such as Excel, that can really help you get on your feet.

2 I've just been promoted and dealing with budgets is a new part of my job. How can I make sure I cut the mustard? I don't have a lot of experience in this area.

If you've just moved into a new position at work, it's a good time to make a pitch for some training. It's perfectly reasonable for you to do so, but to increase the chances of you getting the training you need, make a good business case for it to your manager by explaining the benefits that your company or organisation would derive from it. For example, it may be that:

- you'd be able to hit the ground running and take control of your own budgets early on
- you'd be able to work more efficiently as you wouldn't keep having to check things with the finance department
- you'd be up to speed with the latest software, if appropriate
- you'd be aware of best practice in your given area

Whether you get training or not, don't be afraid to ask other people if you run into any problems. It's much better to query anything you're unsure of than to go off at a tangent, base all your thinking on a mistake, and then have to deal with related problems. If you're polite, to the point, and remember to say 'thank you', you won't go far wrong.

Step two: Understand the key words

Before we go any further, it's a good idea to get to know the key words that are used regularly used in relation to budgets. In most cases, they'll be explained again in their context in each respective chapter, but here is an overview that you can turn to for quick reference:

asset
any item that can have a value assigned to it. Assets can be 'tangible' or 'intangible'. Tangible assets are, as you'd imagine, ones that exist physically, such as machinery, property, and cash. Intangible assets include goodwill and intellectual property; you can't see or touch them, but they bring a lot of value to a business.

balance sheet
a document that tells you something about the financial strength of a business or organisation on the day that the balance sheet is drawn up; it's like a snapshot of something, rather than a film. A balance sheet shows a business's assets (that is, what it owns) and liabilities (that is, what it is owed, or owes to others). The two sides of the balance sheet must be equal.

bottom line

the net profit or loss (in other words, that which is left after all taxes have been paid) that a company makes at the end of a certain period of time.

cash flow

the movement of money through a business that the business has generated by its own operations, rather than what it has borrowed from other sources. Cash flow is an all-embracing term for the money that a business receives from sales (the cash *in*flow) and the money that it pays out (the cash *out*flow).

credit

credit is one of those key financial words that has more than one sense. 'Credit' can mean the amount of money left over when someone owns more than they owe (in financial terms, when they have more assets than liabilities—the amount left over when the liabilities are deducted from the total of the assets is their credit). 'Credit' can also mean an arrangement between a purchaser and a supplier, whereby the supplier lets the purchaser buy what he or she requires but pay for it at a later date.

creditors

a creditor is someone that you owe money to. This could be because you've bought something from them, or it could take the form of an advance that they've given you.

debt

debt is the amount of money owed to a person or

organisation. It is also used to describe money borrowed by a person or organisation to finance activities.

debtors

a debtor is someone who owes you money. If you are a supplier, your customers are debtors until they pay you.

depreciation

depreciation is the difference between the original cost of something and the (usually smaller) price you get when you sell it on. Depreciation is based on the principle that some things lose value with the passage of time. Machinery and vehicles are good examples of this. Some things, however, do not depreciate in accounting terms. These include a company's employees, land, and leased or rented property.

financial year

the twelve-month period for which a company produces accounts. Financial years do not necessarily coincide with calendar years. Most companies based in or trading in the United Kingdom have a financial year that runs from 1st April of one year to 31st March of the next, for example.

goodwill

an intangible asset (see above) of a company that includes factors such as reputation, contacts, and expertise, for which a customer may have to pay a premium. Goodwill is one of those assets that does not exist in any physical form, but which can add a great deal to a company's worth. Goodwill does not normally appear on a balance sheet, for obvious reasons, but it may appear when a company is acquired by another.

gross margin
the difference between the manufacturing cost of something and the price at which it is sold

interest
the rate that a lender charges for the use of loaned money

inventory
the complete stock of a company including component parts, materials, work in progress, and completed items

investment
the deposit of funds in something in order to provide an increase in wealth for a company or individual

invoice
a document that a supplier sends to a customer detailing the costs of products or services supplied and requesting payment for them

liability
a debt or financial obligation for which a person or company is responsible

loss
a financial position in which the costs of an activity are bigger than the income derived from it

margin
the difference between the cost of a product or service and the amount of money gained from selling it

net profit
a company's income as shown in a profit and loss account after all relevant expenses, such as tax, have been deducted

overhead
the indirect recurring costs of running a business. There are two types of overhead:

- **fixed overheads** are costs that stay the same whether sales go up or down, and they include items such as gas and electricity bills, phone line rental, loan repayments and so on
- **variable overheads**, on the other hand, do change and are **directly** linked to sales. If sales increase, so do the variable overheads, while if sales go down, the variable overheads decrease. For example, let's say you run a haulage company. If you get more bookings, your sales go up but so will your variable overheads as you'll need to spend more on petrol, servicing, tyres and so on, as you're on the road more.

payback period
the length of time it will take to earn back the money invested in a project

principal
the original amount of a loan, not including interest, or the original amount of money invested in something

profit
the difference between the selling price and the purchase price of something when the selling price is higher

profit and loss account
the summary record of a company's sales revenues and expenses over a period, providing a calculation of profits and losses over that time

return
the income derived from a particular activity, such as the profit made from an investment

revenue
the income generated by a product or service over a period of time

Step three: Have faith in yourself

The fact that you're reading this book means that you want to help yourself gain a new skill. The fact that your colleagues and managers trust you to deal with numbers is a great compliment; *they* think you can manage, and you can! Read on to find out how.

Common mistakes

✗ You're too scared to ask people when you're unsure about something

Many of us hate asking for help: some people don't want to make a 'nuisance' of themselves, while others don't want to admit that they need help. Whatever your viewpoint, it is fine to ask for help at work if you're not sure about something, particularly if you're new to the job or company. It's much better to solve your queries early on and get things straight in your head than to blunder off down the wrong track.

✗ You think the numbers will look after themselves

If you run your own business, or are thinking of starting one, it's a good idea to find an accountant to help you as the procedures involved can be complicated and legislation (that you'd have to comply with) changes regularly. An accountant will keep you up to speed with new developments so that you can make sure that your business complies.

STEPS TO SUCCESS

✔ It's natural to be nervous if you've never felt that you're good with numbers, but keeping calm is a great first step. Your memory will be better and you'll make fewer mistakes.

✔ Take advantage of new technology that will help you get to grips with this new element to your job.

✔ Ask for training if appropriate, and back up your request with a strong business case.

✔ Don't be afraid to ask colleagues and managers for their help if you get stuck. It's better to ask than to start off on the wrong foot.

✔ Find out more about key finance terms and expressions—often they're nowhere near as complicated as they sound.

✔ Don't give up!

Useful links

BBC Learning:
www.bbc.co.uk/learning/subjects/adult_learning.shtml
Business Link:
www.businesslink.gov.uk

Drawing up a budget for the first time

The very mention of the word 'budget' can cause hackles to rise at work. Many people feel constrained by budgets, thwarted by them, or in thrall to them. Why? Because a lot of what we want to do at work can be scuppered by budgets, or the lack of them. We often hear 'the budget won't stretch', when people don't want to say that we just can't afford something. One thing to remember is that 'budget' has two senses: it can mean a limit within which you have to work, as well as a target you have to aim for.

Here, we'll be looking at the first sense—how to work out how much you have to spend on something (and stick to it). The best way to be able to work within budgets is to understand them more. This will also mean that you can come up with better solutions that may actually allow you to do what you want within the constraints of the money available. As with most activities at work, the key here is planning and preparation. This chapter is aimed at anyone putting together a budget for the first time; in the next chapter, we'll look at more detailed versions.

Step one: Understand why people need to budget

Budgeting sensibly is not being stingy: few people or organisations have a bottomless pit of funds, so budgeting is a way of achieving your goals without bankrupting yourself in the process. It's a way to make sure that work you have done constitutes good value for money.

Step two: Find out all the information you need

Gather everything you need to know about the task at hand. For example, think about:

- the **amount of money** you have to spend. If you're drawing up a budget from scratch, you won't necessarily have this information, but if there is a cash limit that you have to stay within, find out what it is (and if there's any leeway) as soon as you can.
- the **deadline**. If you have a very tight deadline, you may have to engage more people to do the work you need completed, or people may charge you more for a quicker turnround, all of which will bump up the overall spend.

- the **level of work** needed. Is your task or project a specialised one? If so, you'll have to pay someone more than you would normally to do it.
- the **type of work** needed.
- **hidden extras**. These could include postage or shipping costs for something that you need or overtime if you need something turned round quickly.
- **contingency**. See below for more information!

Step three: Work out your priorities

As part of the planning process, you need to work out your priorities for the job at hand. Think about your main objective and then break it down into smaller milestones. For example, let's say that your objective is to equip a new office in your building. You have a budget of £3,500. You need to work out the **must-haves**—essential items that you can't manage without—and the **nice-to-haves**—desirable but not essential items.

Must-haves would include:

- desk
- computer and screen
- good-quality chair
- telephone
- storage

Nice-to-haves would include:

- kettle
- plants

- microwave
- posters/decorations
- sofa/comfortable chairs

There's one final thing to add to the mix, though: contingency. Life being what it is, something is bound to go wrong along the way, which probably means that you'll end up paying more for something that you'd first anticipated. It's a good idea to add a cushion of 10% on to your costs to account for mishaps along the way.

TOP TIP
Remember that if you have a fixed limit to your budget, the contingency still needs to fall *within* that limit.

Step four: Balance the budget

Step three above leads us on to the concept of balancing a budget; in other words, juggling what you spend so that you don't end up going over your limit.

When you're looking after a budget, you need to strike a balance between being constantly vigilant about the details and lifting your head above the parapet to see the whole picture. For example, if you find you over-spend in one area or on one thing, try not to panic—you'll take your eye off the ball and everything will go downhill. Instead, keep calm and work out how you can save money in another area. This will mean that overall, you're still on track.

Using our example above, let's say that you've decided you can only afford the must-haves for the office you're kitting out. The computer costs more than you'd bargained for, so you'll need to spend less on the other items you need in order to come under your budget of £3,500. The contingency will also come in handy here.

It's a good idea to keep track of what you're spending and to keep a note of the real costs of things, as opposed to the costs you'd assumed. A simple table like the one below would do fine. You don't have to have column four, which shows the difference between the actual and the assumed cost—it's just a way of showing how the costs differ so that you can bear them in mind for next time.

Item	Budgeted cost	Actual cost	Difference
desk	£300	£250	−£50
computer and screen	£2000	£2500	+£500
chair	£300	£190	−£110
telephone	£100	£100	n/a
storage	£500	£300	−£200
10% contingency (of budgeted costs added together)	£300	n/a	n/a
Total	**£3,500**	**£3,340**	

TOP TIP

When you're working out your assumed costs, be realistic! If you're buying equipment, for example, do some research beforehand in up-to-date catalogues or with online retailers, so that you have a true idea of an item's price. This is especially important if you work in, or are buying in, a specialist area—there's no point guessing about costs as you could be way off.

Common Mistakes

✗ You rush in

If you're not naturally a 'numbers person', it might seem daunting to cope with budgets at first. Whatever you do, though, try not to rush in and come up with something at short notice in the hope that it'll make the whole process go quicker. It's much better to take your time, be realistic, and do some thorough research so that you feel comfortable and can back up the reasoning behind your budget to anyone who might ask.

✗ You panic

If things don't go to plan, try not to panic. Things are very rarely as bad as they seem. If you're new to budgeting, you'll probably be reporting to someone who you can answer any queries you have. The best thing you can

do is tackle a problem area as soon as you can. Don't
put it off, as you'll only worry about it more and more
as time goes on, and it might be relatively easy to put
it right.

STEPS TO SUCCESS

✔ Whatever the size of the budget you're creating or
working to, gather together all the information you'll need
as soon as you can, and in as much detail as you can.

✔ Be clear about what you're aiming to do, what the
deadline is, and how much you have to spend.

✔ Identify the must-haves and the nice-to-haves.

✔ Make sure you add some contingency to your budget:
this will help if things go awry or turn out to be more
expensive than you'd planned.

✔ If you overspend in one area, don't panic. Try to cut
back in another area to compensate. As long as you
end up within your figure **overall**, you'll be fine.

Useful links

Institute of Credit Management:
www.icm.org.uk
Small Business—Information and Cash Flow:
www.credit-to-cash.com

Understanding different types of budget

Most people need to have a basic grasp of budgets to do their job well. As we saw in Chapter 2, whatever industry you work in, you have to know how much you can spend on the task at hand, stick to it, and deal with unexpected events along the way.

Now you know how to draw up a basic budget, you can move on to understanding the bigger picture: budgeting. Budgeting is simply the name given to the process of working out what you expect to earn and spend in a given period. The size of budget you're likely to come across will depend on your job; if you're a manager in an established company or if you run your own business, working with budgets is not only unavoidable—it's an essential skill.

If you run your own business, this might be the first time you've had to tackle numbers head-on, as it were. Remember that every business needs to plan its spending on the basis of what it expects to receive from sales of its products or services; if you can't track what you're paying out and receiving in, you can't be sure that your business will survive. Working with budgets also allows you to check how the business is doing

from week to week, or month to month; without this check, you can easily overspend. This chapter explains how you can make use of different budgets.

Step one: Understand the uses of a budget

I What can I use a budget for?

Budgets can be used as a type of control system. If budgeting is part of your job, get into the habit of tracking the actual figures for sales and expenses next to the figures that were forecast—this is easy to do in a spreadsheet computer program, such as Excel. If there are substantial differences between the budgeted figures and the actual figures, act as soon as you can to sort out the problem.

For example, if sales are low, you'll need to think about how you might change your marketing strategies to boost them. If you run your own business, this is something for you to think about, but if you work for a larger organization, flag this up for the relevant people with the right expertise.

If sales, on the other hand, are higher than planned, then you might need to re-think your staffing levels or supplies of raw materials, so that you can cope with the rising demand.

Also, if you find you're just spending too much, you'll need to look for ways to bring costs down.

2 How do I estimate sales and expenditure?

The starting point for drawing up a budget is for you to estimate future sales and expenditure. You can split up the sales budget in a variety of ways, but you could divide it up into:

- the number of different products your business plans to sell
- the number of units of each product that you plan to sell
- the price that you plan to sell each unit for

Remember to add in any discounts that you might offer customers, as these may have quite a big impact when taken all together.

Split your expenditure budget into:

- production costs or variable costs (such as materials, power, and subcontractors)
- overhead costs or fixed costs (such as rent and salaries)
- capital costs (such as equipment and the purchase of property)

Read on to Steps two and three for more information on these two budgets.

Step two: Budget for sales

If your business is a new one or if your business is moving into a new product line, forecasting sales will be particularly tricky because you don't have *actual* sales from the past on which you can base your expectations. Instead, you'll have to make sure that your budget is based on good research. It must also be closely tied to a realistic marketing plan that will generate the sales you expect.

TOP TIP

It's important not just to guess your sales figures—if you underestimate, you may find that you run out of stock; if you over-estimate, you'll have a lot less money to spend than you thought and you may over-stretch yourself as a result. Also, don't start by looking at your planned expenditure and then just deriving a sales forecast to cover the cost.

✔ Make the sales budget as detailed as you can. You need to make it very clear what you plan to sell, and at what price.

✔ Set out your expected sales on a monthly or quarterly basis. If your business sells a range of products, make sure that you prepare sales budgets for each of them. If your products are sold in more than one area, then you may find it helpful to have a sales budget for each area.

TOP TIP

It's a good idea to have a sheet of short notes that accompany your budget; sometime these are called 'assumptions'. For anyone else (other than you) looking over the budget for the first time, they'll explain how you've come up with the figures shown. For example, if you need to allow for someone to do some freelance work for you, this may show up as just one line in your budget of £500. In the assumptions sheet, you can elaborate on this and spell out exactly what that cost is made up of—say 20 hours' work at £25 per hour.

Step three: Budget for expenditure

Now that you've thought about your potential income, you have the basic foundations for working out what your expenditure will be (on the basis that you can only spend what you earn!).

For your purposes, the expenditure budget can be split into a production budget and an overheads budget. If you know how many products you'll sell, you can work out the direct costs of producing them. These direct costs will then make up the production budget, and will vary depending on what you're producing and how. The overhead costs, which are explained below, will stay more or less constant.

1 The production budget

The production budget is made up of items like the materials and components that go into making your product. If you have a sales team, you also need to include commission paid to them. If sales people earn a regular retainer as well, this retainer would normally be regarded as a fixed cost. Make sure that you include the cost of subcontractors, where people are being paid as independent contractors to perform a certain, defined job. Discounts are usually shown in the budget as a direct cost.

2 The overheads budget

Once you have worked out the production budget, you'll need to consider the other costs that the business will incur. These will include the salaries for you and your staff, National Insurance contributions, and pension contributions. You'll also need to include rent and company insurance, and telephone, Internet, and e-mail account costs. Any interest on money that you have borrowed will also need to be included in your overheads.

If your business is in manufacturing, it's likely that the above will represent a relatively small proportion of the total costs. On the other hand, if you have a service sector business, it's likely that overheads will represent a very high proportion of the cost.

To get a true picture, then, make sure you include **all** overhead costs, including interest payments and drawings (if you run your own company, this is how much money you plan to take out of the business).

TOP TIP
Your business may aim to allocate the overheads to each product, or may prefer to retain overheads as a single budget. Whichever path you choose, make sure that the price you charged for each product makes a reasonable contribution to the overhead costs incurred in getting it to market.

Step four: Budget for the full cost of production

You're now in a position to pull together the production budget and the overheads budget into a single production cost budget. If there is more than one product or service, then there will be a production budget for each. There will also be variable overheads for you to add for each product (see pp X and Y if you need to refresh your memory about these).

There's no need for you to split fixed overheads across products at this point, since the object of this exercise is for you to be able to determine the total costs.

Capital expenditure budget

If you expect to buy equipment, you'll need to decide how to pay for it (whether in cash or through a loan), and make sure that you budget for these payments in the relevant months. This is essential information if an accurate forecast is to be prepared, particularly where the business may have to take out a loan to finance the purchase and will have to meet a repayment schedule that includes interest.

If the business decides to lease equipment, it's important to make sure that you read all the small print. While the selling is carried out by a supplier, the leasing is done by a finance company and the conditions are inevitably more favourable for them than for your business. On the other hand, the organisation leasing the equipment to you usually has a responsibility to make sure that the equipment keeps working, even if the supplier can no longer support it.

Cash flow

If the business you work for or own operates on a cash basis—that is, taking in cash for your sales and paying out cash for your purchases—it's fairly easy to see whether you're living within your means, as you'll have cash left over at the end of the month if you're making a profit.

Very few businesses operate like this, though. It's far more likely that you'll be selling goods or services in one month, and not receiving payment until the following month, or the month after that. Similarly, you may be buying raw materials one month, but not paying for them for at least another four weeks.

A budget will help you keep track of your cash flow in and out of the business, and keep control. Once the budgets have been prepared, you can use the data that you get from them to that has been accumulated in order to prepare financial forecasts. This will include a cash flow forecast, but you should also include a forecast of the profit and loss statement, and the balance sheet (see Chapters 8 and 9).

The cash flow forecast should set out, on a month-by-month basis, all the cash coming in to and out of the business for the following 12 months, and it will help you work out the funds you need to operate your business. The profit and loss forecast will help you to check that your business remains profitable.

See Chapter 7 for more advice on solving cash-flow problems that may crop up.

Common mistakes

✗ You don't set realistic targets

If you set realistic targets, you'll be able to tell whether sales and expenditure have gone to plan, and you'll also be able to foresee problems and opportunities in time to take action.

✗ You don't bother to do a cash-flow forecast

A cash-flow forecast is as important as the budget itself. While the budget can tell you if your business is generally profitable, it might not alert you to the fact that you may run out of money at crucial times in the year. Looking at the bigger picture is always useful whether you own your business or not.

STEPS TO SUCCESS

✔ Remember that 'budgeting' is simply the name given to the process of working out what you or your business expects to spend and earn in a given period.

✔ Don't be too put off by the idea of budgeting: it's a useful control system to make sure that a business stays on track and doesn't overspend.

✔ Get into the habit of tracking the difference between what you budgeted for and what you actually spent on something; you may spot patterns and this will help you boost your estimation skills for future budgets.

✔ When you work out what your sales figures will be, do plenty of research before coming up with the final number. Don't guess or just fit in any old number that covers all your planned spending either.

✔ Be as detailed as you can in your budgets.

Useful links

Institute of Credit Management:
www.icm.org.uk
Small Business—Information and Cash Flow:
www.credit-to-cash.com

Keeping on top of costs

The basic idea behind a successful business is that you earn more than you spend. One way to boost your profits is to increase the sales of your business, but you can also do it by cutting down on your outgoings. A business that keeps its costs under control will have more funds for growth in the good times and will also be in a better position to survive rainy days. This chapter gives some suggestions on ways to control (and in some cases, reduce) costs at work.

Step one: Work out which costs you need to control

Before you can control your costs, you need to know exactly what they are.

✔ Start by identifying each cost clearly, and make sure that you keep records of all bills, receipts, and so on. If you're self-employed, you'll need to keep all of these for tax purposes anyway. Also if you run your own business, you'll need to factor in staff costs, your own wages, utilities, suppliers' bills, and so on. If you work in someone else's business, you won't have to control the same type of costs, but you'll need to chart what you spend to get your job done.

✔ Review your costs regularly and chart your actual costs against estimated costs so that you can get a better idea of how your budgeting is working.

TOP TIP

If you run your own business, remember that it's not enough to calculate whether the business is in profit or loss; you also need to be aware of what 'normal' costs are so that you can spot anomalies and take action to address them. Some costs will be more important to control than others—you need to know what the business's *critical* costs are and then concentrate on reducing them.

Step two: Realise that everyone can help with cost control

Most people never give it a second thought, but cost control is the responsibility of everyone working in the business, not just those working in the accounts or finance departments.

All employees have countless opportunities to affect costs throughout each day. If you're a manager, remember that people who are unhappy at work are in a position to do a lot of damage, if only as a result of what they *don't* do. If they're motivated and feel part of the business, they'll naturally work in a cost-effective way without having to be supervised.

Rising to the challenge of providing this kind of environment for your employees is a test of good management; one approach is to involve employees by asking them to come up with ideas to reduce costs. If you do decide on this option, though, be careful with the way you phrase this request. Unless the company is in dire straits and you *are* thinking of making redundancies, don't give them the impression that their jobs are on the line as part of this cost-cutting measure!

Staff costs are a big outgoing for businesses of all sizes. When times are tight, staff cuts are often made but before you get to that stage, ask yourself if you're getting the best value from your staff—without taking them for granted. If you put in the time to manage and motivate them well, you'll reap great benefits, so don't forget to look at your own role whether you're an entrepreneur or a manager.

Don't assume either that cutting salaries in lean times will help you weather the storm: while there has to be some limit on what you can pay people, clearly, if you don't pay them the going rate, people will leave and take their knowledge with them, all of which may damage performance in the long run.

TOP TIP

**Many people assume that because the
amounts of money they deal with at work are
so much larger than those they're used to in
home life, any savings they might make are
insignificant. Every little does help, though,
so let your team know that cutting back
on what look like insignificant costs
will help the business overall.**

Step three: Use some cost-control measures

I Cost–benefit analysis

One way to make sure that money is being spent in the right place, and on the right things, is to do a cost–benefit analysis. In broad strokes, this will let you know if the benefits of a particular course of action justify the amount of money spent on it.

For example, a person may be assigned to carry out a piece of research that could, in fact, be done quicker by a consultant, or bought off the shelf. What would be the costs of these latter options, though? If you can't afford to buy in outside help but need the information that the research would produce, it may be worth considering. On the other hand, if the work would only have a small impact on profitability, it might not be worth doing at all.

TOP TIP
**If you have invested a lot emotionally in a
project—if it's your idea, say, or you've been
responsible for it for a long time—it can be
hard to take a step back and look at the pros
and cons pragmatically, but it is important
to do this if you are to keep a grip on costs.**

---

2 Value analysis

Another method of cost control is value analysis (VA), which
involves a detailed examination of each part of a product,
service, or system to work out if there is any way in which
its costs could be reduced without affecting quality. Value
analysis is usually done by a group of people, and as a result,
it's a good way to involve everyone and build up their general
awareness of cost control.

✔ Bring an aspect of the product or project in question
under the spotlight and ask some key questions. For
example:

- is the product/project necessary?
- can it be made with cheaper materials?
- is it cheaper to buy it in than make it?
- can it be simplified to reduce potential faults?

3 Cut down on wastage

Depending on the type of industry you're in, reducing the
wastage of raw materials can really make a difference to your

spending. If you've been doing something a certain way for quite a long time, you might be blithely going down the same old route without considering whether advances made in recent years may mean that you can do things differently, quicker, and cheaper.

If you have your own business or you buy in services for the company you work for:

✔ reassess your purchasing methods

✔ look for discounts for buying in bulk and don't be afraid to haggle

✔ investigate new technologies

You don't have to make a big switch straightaway, but some estimates of how much you might be able to save will be very helpful.

TOP TIP

**Take some time to review the cost of supplies
and suppliers regularly. Check all the bills or
invoices that you receive (as you should your
bank statements) to make sure that there are
no mistakes. Genuine errors can happen, so
it is worth double-checking to be on the
safe side. If a supplier gave you an estimate
before starting a job with you, make sure that
the final bill hasn't gone over your budget.**

---

4 Think about stock control

If the business you own or work in manufactures products, keeping an eye on stock control is another way to potentially save some money. Over-stocking can mean that you pay more than you need to for storage and warehousing, for example, so be realistic about what you need and when you're likely to need it.

TOP TIP

If your business manufactures products that have a high market price (or if you're a wholesaler), do check that you're protecting your stock well. For example, electronic equipment, pharmaceuticals, alcohol, and cigarettes are the type of thing that people might try to steal. Your insurance should cover theft, of course, but it's much better to keep your stock secure so that you don't lose money as a result of someone else's actions.

Step three: Save money and help the environment!

One environmentally-friendly way of making your business run more leanly is to cut down on energy costs.

✔ Encourage your employees to use energy as responsibly at work as they do at home (where *they* are paying the bills). Many people today are concerned about the environment, and this can motivate them to save energy. It's easy to forget that some of the biggest savings available to businesses lie within some of their most basic costs, such as gas and electricity.

✔ Have your meters double-checked, especially if the business uses a lot of energy, and set thermostats correctly. Something as basic as insulation can really help you shrink your bills and produce long-term savings, and you may even be eligible for a grant to help pay for it. The BusinessLink website has a very helpful section on energy efficiency at work under the 'Health, safety and environment' option—see below for the address.

Common mistakes

✗ You make false economies

Don't cut back on the wrong things. If you reduce the level of service your customers are used to, you'll probably end up losing the business money. Similarly, if you make working conditions too harsh, for example, by cutting back on pay, benefits, and training, your staff will become demoralised and will not perform—indeed, you run the risk of them leaving.

✗ You ignore rising costs

Don't stick your head in the sand. Cost problems won't go away, and it's much better to act quickly once you know they're there, so that you can stop the problem from escalating.

STEPS TO SUCCESS

✔ If you need to boost your profits, think about how cutting spending (as well as boosting sales!) can help you out.

✔ If you run your own business, work out exactly which costs it incurs: how long is it since you sat down and went through a month's invoices in any detail?

✔ Realise that everyone in a business can help cut down on costs, whatever their role. Lots of small savings can really add up.

✔ Keep your team motivated. If they don't care about the business, they won't think about how they can help it out of a tight spot.

✔ Before you go ahead with a project, be sure that the benefits justify the cost.

✔ Take a step back from a project you're closely involved in and try not to let your emotional ties to it blind you to ways you can save.

✔ Reassess the way you do things and try to cut down on waste wherever possible.

✔ Review what you're being charged by your suppliers. If you've not negotiated rates for a while, find out about the current market rate and see how you're faring.

✔ Although running out of stock is always something to be avoided, don't go too far the other way and produce too much — you'll spend a fortune on warehousing costs, all of which will eat into your profits.

✔ Save money and protect the environment at the same time by checking whether your business is energy-efficient.

Useful links

Building Research Energy Conservation Support Unit:
www.bre.co.uk
BusinessLink:
www.businesslink.gov.uk/bdotg/action/home

Managing payments to and from a business

Managing payments to and from a business is an essential part of keeping a company afloat, whatever its size. Even if you don't deal with payments directly as part of your job, it's important to know how this aspect of finance management feeds in to the 'bigger picture'. If you own your own business, the need to plug the gaps in your knowledge is an urgent one!

All businesses have trading relationships with both suppliers and customers. At any point in time, those suppliers who are extending credit to your business by letting you pay for goods or services after you have received them, are known as your *creditors.* Customers who owe you money for goods or services that you have supplied to them are known as your *debtors.* The balance between when you need to pay your creditors and when you receive payment from your debtors has a major effect on the cash flow of your business. Getting this balance right is important in determining what cash will be available to your business in the short term, and for identifying the cash needs (often referred to as 'working capital') of your business as it grows.

Step one: Understand why you need to keep an eye on creditors and debtors

1 Why do I need to manage creditors and debtors?

Knowing how much you owe, how much you are owed, and when payments are due to be made or received, allows you to forecast your cash flow over several months. It also means that you can make sure you have enough money in the bank for other regular outgoings, such as salaries and rent. This can be particularly important for businesses that are seasonal, or that spend a lot with their suppliers several months before their customers pay them.

2 How does this affect the cash required by a business?

When the value of your creditors equals the value of your debtors, there is no effect on the working capital needs of your business, assuming payment terms are the same. If the value of your debtors increases relative to the value of your creditors, though, the working capital used by your business rises. This is a typical situation faced by businesses as they grow. If you are able to increase the value of your creditors while maintaining the value of your debtors then you can reduce the working capital needed by your business.

3 What are standard payment terms?

There are no firm rules for credit terms, but there are accepted practices that are widely adopted. Normally the credit period is either based on the date of the invoice, or on the month of the invoice. The most standard credit term based on the date of invoice is 30 days—that is, the invoice is due for payment 30 days after the date on the invoice. If you are providing several invoices to a customer in any one month, it is normal to use 'net monthly terms'. This means that all invoices for a particular month are grouped and paid together at the end of the following month. Using net monthly terms greatly simplifies the process for both supplier and customer, reducing the payment process to only once a month, irrespective of the number of invoices issued.

4 What is debtor finance?

For many businesses, the money owed to them by their debtors is the largest single element of their balance sheet. If your business is trading in a business-to-business environment, you could use the services of a third-party finance company that will make money available to you, based on the security of your debtor balances. This service is called 'factoring' and can range from the provision of just finance against your debtor list to a full sales ledger and credit-control service. The initial advance payment is usually up to 80% of the value of the invoice, with the remaining balance being due either at an agreed maturity date, or when your customer pays the factor. This type of service is especially useful for fast-growing businesses which can suffer from a shortage of working capital.

5 What is creditor finance?

This is the term used for 'borrowing' money from your creditors to fund your working capital. This is done, basically, by paying the people to whom you owe money as late as you can. This is an option typically used by retail businesses, where you sell your products or services for cash, and yet obtain credit from your suppliers. However, while going down this route may solve a cash-related headache in the short term, don't go too far—people will soon get tired of it and your reputation will suffer.

6 Are trade suppliers my only short-term creditors?

Although trade suppliers are usually viewed as being the creditors of your business, you should actually include all of the organisations that you owe money to in the short term. This means that the term 'creditors' is more formally split between trade creditors—which will include your trade suppliers to your business–and other creditors, which will include organisations such as the Inland Revenue, if you are an employer and Customs and Excise if you are VAT registered.

TOP TIP
**Managing your creditors and debtors is vitally
important to the smooth operation of your
business. Whatever the size of the business
you run or work in, it will save you money,
but if you do own your own company, it
may even make the difference between
your business surviving or failing.**

Step two: Manage the relationship with your creditors

Suppliers are vital to the operation of your business and the role that they play is often undervalued. For many suppliers, how you manage the payment of their account is a key to a successful long-term relationship. The main issues for a good working relationship with your suppliers are for you to be:

- **professional** in your handling of their account, by conforming to the agreed credit terms, and not wasting their time through poor administration
- **honest** with them if you have cash-flow problems and are unable to meet their normal payment terms
- **straightforward** in your commercial negotiations— look to negotiate better terms from your suppliers, but base this on the volume of business and how this has

grown over a period of time, and the fact that you manage your account well

If you are finding it difficult to get the credit you need from your suppliers, you could consider using a credit card as a short-term solution to paying for the goods. This option will offer the supplier immediate payment, but also give you 30–50 days credit. However, there can be an additional charge added to the invoice of 1–3%, and it's essential that you pay it off promptly or you will incur further cost.

Step three: Manage the relationship with your debtors

If providing credit to your customers is important to your business, it's vital to set up ways to keep a close eye on it.

✔ Ask your customers to complete an account application form, giving details about their business and its legal structure, and references.

✔ Supply them with a copy of your standard terms and conditions of sale, and make sure they are aware of (and acknowledge) your payment terms and what their credit limit is.

✔ Keep records of quotations and delivery notes. This will mean that if missing information is the source of a payment dispute, you have a good chance of being able to find it.

✔ Send out invoices promptly and follow up with regular statements and reminders.

Whatever the size of the business you work for or run, it's a good idea to monitor your customers' payments. If you're unhappy with them, speak to your regular contact there as well as the finance department—he or she might be able to get things moving more quickly at the other end. If, after all that, the customer still doesn't pay, be prepared to halt supplies and to take further action to collect the debt if necessary. Also consider withdrawing credit facilities from persistently poor payers.

TOP TIP
So that you can easily review how much each business owes to you and how old their debt is, produce a regular debtors list organised in balance order. Concentrate your efforts on those customers who have the oldest and largest debts to make the best use of your time.

Common mistakes

✗ **You concentrate on the wrong things**
Do not focus all of your efforts on getting better payment

---

terms from your creditors at the expense of not managing your debtors more effectively. If your business regularly struggles to pay its creditors because of slow payment from your debtors, this will be an indication that your business does not have sufficient working capital. You will then need to decide if you can manage your debtors better, and reduce the average credit period given, or whether you will need to get additional finance into the business to increase your available working capital.

STEPS TO SUCCESS

✔ Don't just see a sale as something that's done and dusted when you dispatch goods to a customer—you have to make sure they've paid you on time too.

✔ Understand the difference between creditors and debtors. People you owe money to are creditors; people who owe you money are debtors.

✔ Managing creditors and debtors well means that you can plan your cash flow over a certain period of time, and also that you can be sure that you have enough money in the bank to pay bills and salaries.

✔ To build an excellent relationship with your suppliers, make sure that you, your staff, or your colleagues are always professional, honest, and straightforward.

✔ If you run your own business, take great care if you consider using a credit card to pay for something from your suppliers.

✔ If your business provides credit to its customers, ask for references for new customers.

✔ Make sure new customers know your terms and conditions of sale, that they acknowledge them, and that they know what their credit limit is.

✔ To keep a close eye on who owes you what, keep a list of debtors organised in balance order. Chase up those who have the largest and oldest debts first.

Useful links

Better Payment Practice Campaign:
www.payontime.co.uk
Factors and Discounters Association:
www.factors.org.uk

Being paid on time

We all know how frustrating it is when we don't receive payment that we're owed. In business, though, the amounts of money involved are probably much larger than those we deal with in everyday life, and as a result, so are the related problems. Whether you run your own company or you work for someone else's, late payments can throw your cash flow into all types of disarray and can cause significant problems. To keep on top of things, you need to make sure that you're issuing invoices properly and chasing late payers.

Basically, when your business supplies goods or services to its customers, you need to record these transactions formally with an invoice. This document becomes particularly important when you let your customers defer payment for the transaction by offering them credit. From the date that the invoice is issued until it is paid, the value of the invoice is regarded as a debt to the business. This chapter explains the invoicing procedure and offers advice on how to deal with customers who don't (or won't) pay up on time.

Step one: Understand more about invoices

1 Why do I need to issue invoices?

An invoice is a formal record of trading between two parties. It confirms details of the goods or services supplied, and the prices charged. It's used as the basis for all financial management and accounting processes in a business, and is a key document in business tax records. An invoice issued by your business to confirm a sale is also a crucial document for the customer, as it acts as proof of purchase.

2 Are there different types of invoices?

Yes. Three types of invoice can be issued:

- **pro-forma invoice.** This type of invoice is issued by a business when it does not have credit facilities set up with its customer, and it acts as a request for payment for goods before they're dispatched. This system makes sure that payment is received upfront, and it's often used when two businesses haven't traded with each other before.
- **standard invoice.** A standard document issued to confirm a trading transaction, this type of invoice can have a variety of names depending on the issuer and recipient. For example, it's normally called a 'sales invoice' by the business that has sold the goods, and as a 'purchase invoice' by the buyer. When an invoice is

issued by a VAT-registered business, it is known as a VAT invoice. It must provide specific information about the rate and amount of VAT charged.

■ **credit note.** This is issued to cancel an original invoice or part of an invoice when goods are returned, a pricing error has been made, or fees have been renegotiated. If the original invoice has been settled prior to the credit note being issued, then the buyer will be entitled to alternative goods up to the value of the credit note.

3 What details should be included on an invoice?

All invoices need to contain certain key pieces of information to act as supporting evidence for tax and VAT purposes, and to avoid queries from customers which may lead to delays in payment. These are:

■ a unique identifying number
■ your business name, address, its legal status, and VAT number (if you're registered for VAT)
■ a date of issue (this becomes the tax point)
■ your customer's name (or trading name) and address
■ a description of the quantity and type of goods or services supplied, along with the price charged, and, where appropriate, the VAT charged
■ the payment terms for the invoice

4 Do invoices always have to be issued?

You don't always need to issue your customers with invoices, but you do need to keep a record of the transaction. For example, many retail businesses issue till receipts to their customers rather than fully-detailed invoices, and this is fine for small, one-off transactions that are paid for at the time of purchase. Most business-to-business transactions require an invoice to be issued, though, and this is especially important if you and your customer are VAT-registered.

5 What can I do if the customer won't pay?

It's important to find out as soon as you can *why* your customer won't pay the invoice. If it's a simple issue, such as a genuine query or error about the price or quantity of something, it should be reasonably simple to sort out. If you need to chase a customer, send a letter (and keep a copy) to find out what the problem is. Keep copies of any further letters or e-mails that you send and also keep a note of any phone calls you have with the customer; all of these records will help if you need to take more formal action.

If this looks unavoidable—if, say, your customer gives you a reason for non-payment that you find unacceptable and you can't reach a compromise—you clearly need to take some steps to retrieve the money you're owed, such as:

■ instructing a solicitor to pursue the debt for you. This may just involve him or her sending a letter on your behalf, or managing the whole process of pursuing your claim through the court process.

■ engaging the services of a debt collection agency, who will either manage the process for a fixed fee, or work on a commission of a percentage of the debt that is collected

■ as a last resort, using the County Courts and the small claims procedure for debts of less than £5,000

Before you start the ball rolling on any of these approaches, you need to weigh up if it's actually worth it; balance the time that it will take for you to pursue your customer for payment against the costs involved with using the services of a solicitor or debt collection agency.

TOP TIP

If you'd like to find an alternative way of solving a dispute, you could try finding a mediator or arbitrator to help find a way forward (and hopefully make your errant customer pay!). Visit the Chartered Institute of Arbitrators' website for more advice—their address appears at the end of the chapter.

Step two: Set up credit control procedures

If you offer credit to your customers, then the issuing of a sales invoice is just part of the sales process, and the transaction is not completed until the invoice has been fully settled. Many businesses are very successful at selling their goods or services and yet still fail because they are unable to collect the money owed to them. It's vital, therefore, to set up processes that minimise the risk of your customers failing to pay you. Make sure that credit is only offered to credit-worthy customers, and that you agree payment terms with them in advance.

✔ Check the accuracy of invoices before you send them out, and provide customers with monthly statements showing their account balance. When credit terms are exceeded, send reminder letters and follow up with telephone calls, and be prepared to put a customer's account on hold if there is no good reason for non-payment. Finally, don't be afraid to charge interest under the Late Payment of Commercial Debts (Interest) Act 1998.

In July 2004, UK businesses struggling with late payers were given an extra boost by the government when the interest chargeable on overdue payments went up: you can now charge an extra 8% on top of the Bank of England base rate. This rate is discussed and set by the Bank every month and it can stay the same, go up, or go down. As a result, there's no hard and fast rule about what you can charge, but if, say, the rate is at 4.5% in the month you decide to charge someone for not paying on time, you can now charge a total of 12.5% interest.

Let's look at a worked example. If someone owes you
£1,000, this would mean:

$$£1,000 \times 0.125 = \textbf{£125} \text{ interest to be charged}$$

Step three: Investigate non-payment

Sometimes, despite all your efforts, you'll still end up with
some people who won't pay on time. You'll then have
to decide on the best way to recover your debt. The
approach you use will depend on your customer,
their size and importance to your business, and the
size of the debt. There are several reasons for
non-payment.

■ **habitual slow payer.** Sometimes new customers are
won suddenly, and it is only after you've supplied them
for a while that you find out why: their previous supplier
had closed their account because they were continually
late with their payments. These types of customers will
go through long delaying tactics as a matter of course,
and can waste a huge amount of your (or your finance
department's) time in chasing them. Undertaking credit
checks can help to minimise this risk, but often it's only
by adopting very tight credit control and setting low
credit limits initially that you can limit the problem. If the
problems continue you may then have to decide
between charging higher prices to reflect your extra
costs, or refusing to give your customer credit.

- **disputed invoices.** Misunderstandings about the terms of a transaction are quite common, and the easiest way to avoid them is to make sure that each stage of the sales process has been documented. If this information is not complete, you may have to face negotiating a compromise with your customer, which could mean that you get paid for only part of the invoice. If there is no room for compromise and you believe that your case is strong, then you should look at formal recovery of your debt as the best way forward—although the process can be time-consuming and expensive. If the dispute does end up in court, you'll need to be able to demonstrate that you have explored all avenues to resolve it, so you should document the process carefully.
- **financial difficulty.** This is probably the most common reason for non-payment of an invoice, and is often masked by your customer behind lots of other reasons. You need to identify whether this is a short-term cash-flow glitch or a major financial problem that is likely to result in your customer becoming insolvent. In situations where a customer faces a short-term difficulty, it may be possible to agree to payments by instalment over a specific period. If you do agree to this approach, make sure you confirm it in writing and then monitor the situation carefully to ensure that your customer maintains these special payments. If a customer's business faces long-term or extreme cash-flow problems it is likely to be unable to pay your debt. Knowing the legal status of your customer's business is important under these circumstances, because this will

determine how you can pursue the recovery of your debt. Often the best that you can hope for is that you can claim title to the goods that you have supplied, which may still have some value to you. For this reason, make sure that a retention-of-title clause is used in all of your terms of sale and all invoices which involve the sale of goods.

Common Mistakes

✗ You're too sympathetic to customers' financial problems
If there's no valid reason for non-payment, don't delay the process of debt collection because you're worried about upsetting your customer. This may just lead to your business being owed more, and possibly not getting paid at all if the customer's business ceases trading.

STEPS TO SUCCESS

✔ Don't put off chasing late payers, or feel that you're being a 'nuisance'. A sale is only complete when the goods have been paid for, and the longer you leave it, the more difficult it will be to make the other party pay up.

✔ Always keep records of transactions, whether you issue invoices or not.

✔ If a customer won't pay, find out why. It may be a relatively simple matter that can be sorted out.

✔ Keep records of all chasing e-mails, letters, faxes, and telephone calls you have with the tardy payer.

✔ If your customer repeatedly refuses to pay, think about using a solicitor, debt collection agency, or even the County Courts and the small claims procedure to retrieve what you're owed.

✔ Weigh up which debt collection approach would work best for your business, and what you can afford.

✔ Try arbitration to settle the matter.

✔ Make sure that you only offer credit to credit-worthy customers in the first place! Take up references, be clear about your payment terms, and make sure customers are prepared to go along with them.

Useful links

Chartered Institute of Arbitrators:
www.arbitrators.org
User's guide to the Late Payment Act 1998:
www.payontime.co.uk

Solving cash-flow problems

Whatever the size of business you work in, running out of cash is a real worry. It's particularly dangerous for small businesses—in fact, it's the biggest single cause of them failing. There are many potential reasons behind a cash crisis, but if you take time to understand them, you'll be equipping yourself with the know-how to prevent a short-term problem turning into a much bigger nightmare.

Step one: Understand the factors that have an impact on cash flow

1 How does the behaviour of customers affect cash flow?

Slow payment by customers is a main cause of cash-flow problems for a business. A sale is only completed when an invoice is paid in full, but many businesses concentrate on generating new sales and don't think to set up the credit-control procedures that will make sure they're paid on time until they actually run into problems. It's much safer to have these in place early on so that you don't get caught on the hop.

You can also run into problems if a key customer becomes insolvent. If your business is dependent on a few major customers (this is a common issue for start-up companies, and is sometimes called the 'Marks & Spencer syndrome' as M&S often insisted on being a company's major or even sole customer), you're always exposed to the risk of one of them having their own financial problems, which could result in you not getting paid. This could be disastrous if the income from that client makes up a big chunk of your overall revenue and you are relying on that money to pay your creditors or employees.

2 How does poor planning affect cash flow?

Poor financial planning can cause businesses to come unstuck. All businesses have to plan for certain outgoings, build them into their cash-flow forecasts, and then make sure that sufficient funds will be available at key times. For example, you'd need to schedule the purchase of equipment for when your cash position is stronger, or arrange for the payment to be structured over a longer period to reduce its impact on your cash flow.

Focusing on turnover and neglecting profit can also lead to a cash-flow crisis. A business is only able to generate a *positive* cash flow by generating profits from its trading activities. If you prioritise the turnover of your business, you may improve sales but this might lead to spending more than you earn (a problem known as *negative* cash flow). This can be a particular problem if the business has to invest in new equipment and staff as it grows, as these costs are often incurred well in advance of you receiving your additional sales revenue.

Poor planning of purchases is another common reason for cash-flow problems. It can be very tempting to over-commit, especially as many suppliers will offer you discount incentives to purchase larger quantities of their goods; on the face of it, this could look very attractive because it holds the promise of making you a larger profit. You do need to think carefully before committing to large orders of stock, though, particularly while you are establishing your business. If you order bulk purchases and then the items quickly go out of fashion or have a short shelf life, you can be left with stock that you cannot sell but which you still have to pay for.

3 How does the rate of a business's growth affect cash flow?

A lack of working capital can also cause a cash-flow crisis. This means that there is not enough money initially invested in the business to allow it to operate effectively on a day-to-day basis. Businesses can also run into trouble when they grow rapidly and then need to produce more than normal without having the income to fund that growth; this is called over-trading.

Step two: Plan properly

Preparing a realistic cash-flow forecast and then putting it to good use is the basis for avoiding many cash-flow problems.

As it involves working out income and expenditure, working out the forecast should allow you to flag up potential crises before they occur.

Cash-flow forecasts also allow you to do a 'sensitivity analysis', in which you can test out the effects of a number of 'what-if' scenarios, whether it be a period of lower sales or your customers taking longer than normal to pay you. Again, this allows you to be better informed about what strains your business can 'stand'.

A cash-flow forecast normally has three sections:

1 money coming **in to** the business—from sales or loans, for example. If the products or services you supply incur VAT, do remember to add that in too

2 money going **out of** the business—your payments to suppliers and utility bills, for example

3 balances—the sum of monies coming in minus those going out—you can do a monthly balance for a short-term view of things and/or a cumulative balance that will give you the 'bigger' picture

To work out the figures you need to slot into these three categories, you need to estimate budgets for sections 1 and 2. These will give you an idea of when you will receive income from sales and when you'll have to spend on your expenses.

TOP TIP
For a cash-flow forecast to be of any use to
your business, you really have to be realistic!
You'll get a completely skewed picture
otherwise that just won't help at all.

A simple spreadsheet in a package such as Excel can help
you lay out all the figures in an easy-to-read format. Planning
ahead will show you when you need to take it as easy as you
can on the spending front and not commit yourself to any
unforeseen purchases unless it's an emergency (if some
machinery breaks, for example).

TOP TIP
As you'll be preparing a cash-flow forecast in
advance, you'll be using your 'best guess'
when you start off. As the months go by,
though, it's a good idea to update the
statement with 'actuals'—you'll then have
an even clearer picture of how you're doing.

It's a good idea to ask for a second or third opinion on
your cash-flow forecast from colleagues. It can be hard
to think of absolutely everything that might crop up in
terms of income and expenditure, and you can get too
close to a document you've created. It's very helpful
to have the advice of someone who has a bit more
distance.

Step three: Develop good relationships with suppliers and customers

One way to avoid cash-flow nightmares is to set up tight credit-control procedures. It's worth putting in place methods of managing the whole process of giving your customers credit.

✔ Start by only giving credit to approved customers— you're perfectly within your rights to ask for a reference from their other suppliers before you agree to supply them. Check when their accounts are due for payment and make sure that they pay according to your agreed terms.

✔ Also make sure that you have efficient administration procedures for raising your invoices promptly and sending statements to your customers. In this way, you won't be adding to potential delays.

✔ Offering incentives for early payment is another good way to encourage your customers to pay more quickly. You could do this by offering a discount if they either pay on delivery, or within a certain number of days (typically between 7 and 14 days) from the invoice date.

Step four: Get help if you need it

If the business you run or work for is growing rapidly, it might benefit from investigating the option of 'debtor finance'. This means using the services of an invoice discounter or factoring company. These companies enter into an arrangement where they will provide a business with an advance (usually 80%) on the value of your invoices due to be paid, as soon as these invoices are raised.

TOP TIP
Interest is charged by invoice discounters and factoring companies on the balance drawn and there is normally also a service charge, so it's extremely important to look into these costs very carefully to check that they won't actually do you more harm than good.

Factoring companies can also take control of collecting payments from your customers directly, which can save you the costs of using your own staff to manage this process. An agreed overdraft facility with your bank also allows you to borrow money as and when required, up to an agreed limit. It is a relatively cheap way to finance working capital if you have large variations in cash flow during the course of a month (or if your business is very seasonal), because you only pay interest on the amount actually borrowed. If you're continually relying on your overdraft, though, it can be expensive; more importantly, it may also highlight that your business needs additional working capital, or a longer-term form of finance.

With an overdraft, you're also exposed to the risk of 'repayment on demand', which means that your lender can ask for full repayment at any time; a 'term loan' with fixed monthly instalments is safer from your point of view, as the lender can usually only demand full repayment if you default on your instalments. If your business needs to invest in new equipment, but does not have the cash, then you can look to fund this with asset financing, in the form of a term loan, a hire purchase loan, or a leasing deal. This avoids the large cash outflow on the full price of the equipment, and gives you a fixed level of repayment over a set period (usually between two and five years). In situations where the asset is being used as security for the finance, you'll probably still need to provide at least a 10% deposit.

Common mistakes

✗ **You don't think ahead**
Don't be taken by surprise. Keep a close eye on your bank balance and your debtors' book and look ahead to see what you'll be paying out over the next few weeks. Cash-flow problems are best caught early, and the more time you can give yourself to respond, the better.

✗ **You put things off**
Don't be fooled into thinking that cash-flow problems will

resolve themselves; they won't go away! Talk to your bank and your suppliers as soon as you think there might be a problem. This way, you assure them that you are at least doing your homework, even if there are difficult times ahead. If you don't act, you run the risk of affecting your relationship with your bank, suppliers, and customers. Your bank will be far more receptive to dealing with your cash-flow problems if you approach it before the problem occurs.

STEPS TO SUCCESS

✔ Managing cash flow is an important part of any business, but if you run your own small business, it's even more crucial: running out of cash is the main reason for small business failures.

✔ Understand the factors that have an impact on cash-flow. Late payment by customers, bad planning, and the rate that a business grows can all cause havoc.

✔ Preparing a cash-flow forecast is time very well spent. It lists money coming in to and out of the business and the balance, so that you can see exactly where you are — and when problems may crop up.

✔ Be realistic! There's no point spending hours planning and forecasting if you're not honest with yourself.

✔ Ask a colleague to give you his or her opinion on any cash-flow forecasts that you put together. It's easy to get too 'close' to a document you've created and you may miss out some key elements. Some feedback is always useful.

✔ Setting up good credit-control procedures will help you stave off cash-flow nightmares. Give credit only to approved customers, raise invoices promptly, and offer incentives to early payers.

✔ Investigate the option of using debtor finance if you do run into difficulty.

Useful links

Institute of Credit Management:
www.icm.org.uk
Small Business—Information and Cash Flow:
www.credit-to-cash.com

Reading a balance sheet

One essential step in getting to grips with budgets is to understand some of the documents related to them. At first glance, they can seem like meaningless lists of figures, but with practice, you'll see that they can actually tell you a lot about the state a business is in currently and how it may perform in the future.

Let's start with a balance sheet. Balance sheets tell us something about the financial strength of a business on the day that the balance sheet is drawn up. That situation changes constantly, so it's more like a snapshot of something than a film. Although the method of producing a balance sheet is standard, there can be a certain element of subjectivity in interpreting it. Different elements of the balance sheet can tell you different things about how the business is doing.

This chapter gives an overview of the elements that make up a balance sheet and looks at a brief selection of the more interesting figures that help with interpreting one. Remember that a lot of these figures do not tell you much in isolation; it's only as a result of analysing trends or making comparisons between businesses that their message becomes clearer.

Step one: Understand what a balance sheet is (and what it *isn't*)

A balance sheet is an accountant's view of the book value of the assets (credits) and liabilities (debts) of a business at a specific date, and *on that date alone*. The term 'balance' means exactly what it says—that those assets and liabilities will be equal. In showing how the balance lies, the balance sheet gives us an idea of the financial health of the business.

A balance sheet is not designed to represent how much a business would be worth if it were to be sold. For example, property in the balance sheet may be worth a lot more than its book value estimated. Plant and machinery is shown at cost less depreciation, but that may well be different from market value. Stock may turn out to be worth less than its balance-sheet value, and so on. Also there may be hidden assets, such as goodwill or valuable brands, that do not appear on the balance sheet at all. These would all enhance the value of the business in a sale situation, yet are invisible on a normal balance sheet.

Step two: See how the elements fit together

Here is an example of a simple balance sheet:

		£
Fixed assets		1,000
Current assets	700	
Less current liabilities	400	
Net current assets		300
		1,300
Less long-term loans	200	
Net assets		1,100
Profit and loss account		500
Share capital		600
Shareholders' funds		1,100

The elements shown on the balance sheet are the following:

1 **Fixed assets.** These are items that are not produced, bought, or sold as part of a company's normal activities but which allow it to function. Examples include property, machinery, or vehicles—these are *tangible* assets (meaning you can kick them). Under this heading on the balance sheet you'll also find *intangible* assets (which you cannot kick). These include intellectual property and goodwill, both of which are important to the 'bigger picture', especially if an acquisition is in the offing.

2 **Current assets.** These items make up the trading cycle of a business and the most common examples are stock, debtors, and positive bank balances.

3 **Current liabilities.** These are also items that form the trading cycle of the business, but they represent amounts

of money that are owed to others in the short-term. For example, they could be taxes and bank overdrafts—broadly speaking, they're any amount due for payment within the next 12 months from the date of the balance sheet.

4 **Net current assets (NCA).** This is not a new element, but simply the difference between current assets and current liabilities, often shown because it may be a useful piece of information. Ideally, the difference should be a positive figure.

5 **Long-term loans.** These are made up of debt that is repayable more than one year from the date of the balance sheet.

6 **Net assets.** Again, these are not new elements, but the sum of fixed assets *plus* net current assets *less* long-term loans. In other words, all of the company assets shown in its books, minus all of its liabilities.

7 **Profit and loss account.** This is the total of all the accumulated profits and losses from all the accounting periods since the business started. It increases or decreases each year depending on the net profit or loss in that period, calculated after taking into account all costs including tax and dividends to shareholder.

8 **Share capital.** This is the number of shares issued, multiplied by their nominal value. The latter is the theoretical figure at which the shares were *originally*

issued and has nothing to do with their market value (that is, what they can be sold for now).

9 **Shareholders' funds.** Again, not a new figure, but the sum of the profit and loss account plus the share capital. It represents the total interest of the shareholders in the company.

Step three: Learn to interpret balance sheets

Balance sheets differ between one industry and another in terms of the range and type of assets and liabilities that exist. For example, a retailer will have little in the way of trade debtors because it sells for cash, or a manufacturer is likely to have a far larger investment in plant (that is, machinery or equipment) than a service business like an advertising agency. The interpretation of a balance sheet, then, must be seen in the light of the actual trade of the business.

Reading a balance sheet can be quite subjective and although the method of producing a balance sheet is standardised, there may be some items in it that are subjective rather than factual. The way people interpret some of the figures will also vary, depending on what they wish to achieve and their own perspective on whether something is 'good' or 'bad'.

1 Look first at the net assets/shareholders' funds

Positive or negative? Our example, being a healthy business, has net assets of a positive £1,100. Positive is good. If there were 600 shares in issue, it would mean that the net assets per share were £1.83 (1,100 divided by 600).

If it had negative assets (same thing as net liabilities), this might mean that the business is heading for difficulty unless it is being supported by some party such as a parent company, bank, or other investor. When reading a balance sheet with negative assets, ask yourself where the support will be coming from.

2 Look next at net current assets

Positive or negative? Again, our example business has net current assets of a positive £300. This means that, theoretically, it should not have any trouble settling short-term liabilities because it has more than enough current assets to do so. Negative net current assets would suggest that the business may have a problem in settling short-term liabilities.

3 Understand the significance of trade debtor payments . . .

Within current assets, we have trade debtors. It can be useful to consider how many days' worth of sales are tied up in debtors and you can calculate this by multiplying debtors by 365 and dividing by annual sales. This provides an idea of the average time a company is waiting to get paid. Too long, and it might be something requiring investigation. However, this figure can be misleading where sales do not take place evenly throughout the year. A construction company might be an example of such a business: one big debtor near the year end would skew the ratio.

4 . . . and trade creditor payments

Similar to the above, this looks at how long the company is taking in general to pay its suppliers. The basic way of working this out is to multiply trade creditors by 365 and then divide by annual purchases.

This is not so easy to calculate because the purchases for this purpose include not only goods for resale but all the overheads as well.

Step four: Recognise what debt means

This figure is the total of long- and short-term loans. Too much debt might indicate that the company would have trouble, in a downturn, in paying the interest. It's difficult to give an optimum level of debt because there are so many different situations, depending on a huge range of circumstances.

Often, instead of an absolute figure, debt is expressed as a percentage of shareholders' funds (calculated by dividing debt by shareholders' funds and multiplying by 100) and known as 'gearing' or 'leverage'.

Common mistakes

✗ **You believe that balance sheet figures tell you how much a business is worth**
Don't assume that a balance sheet represents a proper valuation of a business. Its primary purpose is that it forms part of the range of accounting reports used for measuring business performance—along with the other common financial reports like profit and loss accounts and cash-flow statements. Management, shareholders, and others such as banks will use the entire range to assess the health of the business.

✗ **You forget that the balance sheet is valid only for the date at which it is produced**
A short while after a balance sheet is produced, things could be quite different. In practice, there usually won't be any radical changes between the date of the balance sheet and the date when it is being read, but it is entirely possible that something could have happened to the business that would not show—a major debtor could have defaulted unexpectedly, for example. Bear in mind, then, that balance sheet figures are valid only as at the date shown, and are not a permanent picture of the business.

STEPS TO SUCCESS

✔ A balance sheet is a 'snapshot' of a business on a given day.

✔ It shows what is owed to the business, and what that business owes to others.

✔ A balance sheet doesn't show how much a business is worth, so don't see it as a valuation tool—remember, it relates to one day **only**.

✔ Although balance sheet formats are standardised whatever industry you're in, balance sheets can differ from industry to industry in terms of the range and type of assets and liabilities they show.

✔ Reading a balance sheet can be subjective, as can the interpretation of the figures; different people may draw different conclusions depending on what their goals are.

Useful link

Biz/ed:
www.bized.ac.uk/learn/business/accounting/busaccounts/notes/bs.htm

Reading a profit and loss account

Just like the balance sheet we encountered in the previous chapter, a profit and loss account (P & L) is a standard financial document that you may have to get to grips at work. It is a statement of how much a business earns and spends over a given period, and is normally drawn up to see how much profit the business has made. If you run your own business, this is a document you'll need to be familiar with, and if you were thinking of acquiring another business, you'd want to closely inspect the P & L of the target company.

Put simply, the difference between the income from sales and any associated expenditure is the profit or loss for the period. 'Income' and 'expenditure' here mean only those amounts that can be allocated directly to earning the profit, and so as a result don't include expenditure on unrelated items that the business still has to pay for, such as property or equipment. Importantly, the figures are adjusted to match the income and expenses to the time period in which they were incurred—which isn't necessarily the same as that in which the cash changed hands.

Step one: Know what profit and loss account shows (and what it *doesn't*)

1 What is a profit and loss account?

A profit and loss account is an accountant's view of the figures that show how much profit or loss a business has made over a given period of time. To do this, various elements of income and expenditure are allocated to the time period concerned, not on the basis of when cash was received or spent, but on when the income was earned or the liability to pay a supplier and employees was incurred. While capital expenditures (that is, money spent on items such as plant or machinery) are excluded, depreciation (or loss of value) of property and equipment is included as a non-cash expense. If you sell goods on credit, then, you'll be paid later but for the purposes of the P & L, the sale takes place upon the contract to sell them. Equally if you buy goods and services on credit, the purchase takes place when you contract to buy them, not when you when you actually settle the invoice.

2 What does a profit and loss account *not* show?

Probably the most important thing to know about a P & L account is that it's definitely **not** an explanation of the cash coming into and going out of a business.

Below is a simple example of a profit and loss account for a particular year.

	£	£
Sales		1000
Opening stock	100	
Purchases	520	
	620	
Closing stock	80	
Cost of sales		540
Gross profit		460
Wages	120	
Other overheads	230	
		350
Net profit before tax		110
Tax		22
Net profit after tax		88
Dividends		40
Retained profit		48
Retained profit brought forward		150
Retained profit carried forward		198

TOP TIP

We can tell that the business is trading or manufacturing goods of some kind as 'stock' and 'purchases' appear on the P & L.

---

3 Why are profit and loss accounts important?

Reading a P & L is the easiest way to tell if a business has made a profit or loss during a given month or year. The most important figure it contains is net profit—this is what is left over after expenses and taxes have been paid.

4 How often are profit and loss accounts prepared?

Companies typically issue P & Ls monthly. It's customary for the reports to include year-to-date figures, as well as corresponding year-earlier figures to make comparisons and analysis easier.

Step two: Define the individual elements

1 **Sales.** The invoiced value of the sales in the period.

2 **Stock.** The value of the actual physical stock held by the business at the opening and closing of the period. It is always valued at cost value, not the selling price.

3 **Purchases and other direct costs.** The cost of goods or raw materials purchased by the business to be sold on elsewhere (this is often referred to as 'resale').

Where a business holds stock, the purchase figure has to be adjusted for the opening and closing values in order to reach the right income and expenditure amounts for that period only. Goods for resale bought in the period may not have been used during that period but may be lying in stock at the end of it, ready for sale in the next. Similarly, goods used for resale in this period will consist partly of items already held in stock at the beginning of it. So take the amounts purchased, add the opening stock and deduct the closing stock. The resulting adjusted purchase figure is known as 'cost of sales'.

In some businesses there may be other direct costs apart from those included in cost of sales. For example, a manufacturer may include some wages if they are of a direct nature (such as wages of employees directly involved in the manufacturing process, as distinct from office staff). Or a building contractor would include plant hire in direct costs, as well as purchases of materials.

4 **Gross profit.** This is the difference between sales and cost of sales. (Cost of sales is the sum of all the costs that go in to a product being sold, including manufacturing and staff costs.) This is an important figure as it measures how much was actually made directly from whatever the business is selling, before it starts to pay for overheads. The figure is often expressed as a percentage ratio, when it is known as the 'gross profit margin' (GPM).

5 **Overheads.** The expenses of the business which do **not** vary directly with sales. They include a wide range of items such as rent, most wages, advertising, phones, interest paid on loans, and so on.

6 **Net profit before tax.** The result of deducting total overheads from gross profit. This is what the business has made before tax is paid on that profit.

7 **Tax (or corporation tax).** This will not actually have been paid in the year concerned, but is shown because it is due on the profit for that period. Even then the figure shown may not be the actual amount due, for various reasons such as possible overpayments from previous years. Tax can be a very complex matter, being based upon a set of changeable rules, so always take expert advice on it.

8 **Net profit after tax.** The result after deducting the tax liability—the so-called 'bottom line', at last! This is the amount that the company can do with as it wishes, possibly paying a dividend out of part of it and retaining the rest. It is the company's reward for actually being in business in the first place.

9 **Dividends.** A payment to the shareholders as a reward for their investment in the company. Most publicly listed companies of any size pay dividends to shareholders. Private companies may also do so, but this may be more for tax reasons. The dividend in the example shown is paid out of the net profit after tax, but legally it is not

permitted to exceed the total available profit. That total available profit is comprised of both the current year's net profit after tax and the retained profit brought forward from previous years.

10 **Retained profit.** The amount kept by the company **after** paying dividends to shareholders. If there is no dividend, then the retained profit is equal to the net profit after tax.

11 **Retained profit brought forward.** The total accumulated retained profits for all earlier years of the company's existence.

12 **Retained profit carried forward.** The above figure carried forward, plus the current year's retained profit. This new total will form the profit brought forward in the next accounting period.

Step three: Interpret the figures

A lot of accounting analysis is valid only when comparing the figures, usually with similar figures for earlier periods, projected future figures, or other companies in the same business. On its own a P & L account tells you only a limited story, though there are some standalone facts that can be derived from it. What our example does show, even in isolation, is that this business was successful in the period concerned. It made a profit, not a loss, and was able to pay dividends to shareholders out of that profit. Clearly a pretty crucial piece of information. However, it is in comparisons that such figures start to have real meaning. The example figures reveal that the gross profit margin was 46%, an important statistic in measuring business performance. The net profit margin before tax was 110:1,000, or 11%. You could take the margin idea further and calculate the net profit after tax ratio to sales as 88:1,000, being 8.8%. Or you could calculate the ratio of any expense to sales.

In our example, the wages:sales ratio is 120:1,000 or 12%. If you then looked at similar margin figures for the preceding accounting period, you would learn something about this business. Say the gross margin was 45% last year compared with 46% this year—there has been some improvement in the profit made before deducting overheads. But then suppose that the net profit margin of 8.8% this year was 9.8% last year. This would tell you that, despite improvement in profit at the gross level, the overheads have increased disproportionately. You could then check on the ratio of each of the overheads to sales to see where this arose and find out why. Advertising spending could have shot up, for example, or perhaps the company moved to new premises incurring a higher rent. Maybe something could be tightened up.

Another commonly used ratio

Another ratio often used in business analysis is return on capital employed. Here we combine the profit and loss account with the balance sheet by dividing the net profit (either before or after tax as required) by shareholders' funds. This tells you how much the company is making proportionate to money invested in it by the shareholders—a similar idea to how much you might get in interest on a bank deposit account. It's a useful way of comparing different companies in a particular industry, where the more efficient ones are likely to derive a higher return on capital employed.

Common Mistakes

✗ You assume that the bottom line represents cash profit from trading

It doesn't! There are a few examples where this is the case: a simple cash trader might buy something for one price, then sell it for more; his profit then equals the increase in cash. But a business that buys and sells on credit, spends money on items that are held for the longer term, such as property or machinery, has tax to pay at a later date, and so on, will make a profit that is not represented by a mere increase in cash balances held. Indeed, the cash balance could quite easily decrease during a period when a profit was made.

STEPS TO SUCCESS

✔ A profit and loss account (P & L) is an accountant's view of the figures that show how much profit or loss a business has made over a given period of time.

✔ Remember that a P & L doesn't show how a business earned or spent its money.

✔ Keep the bigger picture in mind when you read a P & L: one month's figures may be misleading in isolation, particularly if a business generates most of its receipts in a particular month. For example, retail businesses generate most of their sales in the last three months of the year, in the run-up to Christmas. Consultancies, on the other hand, might generate the lion's share of their revenues in as few as two months, and no revenues at all in some other months.

✔ Analysing P & Ls is a very subjective matter. Two people may read the same one and reach different conclusions, depending on what their agenda is.

Useful link

The Motley Fool UK:
www.fool.co.uk

Where to find more help

Book-keeping & Accounting for the Small Business: How to Keep the Books and Maintain Financial Control Over Your Business
Peter Taylor
Oxford: How To Books, 2003
192pp ISBN: 1857038789
Aimed at both students and anyone running or responsible for the accounts of a small business, this guide offers structured advice on the essentials of book-keeping.

Finance for the Non Specialist
Janet Walker
London: CIMA Publishing, 1998
166pp ISBN: 1874784736
This introductory text is designed for non-specialist managers and students who need an understanding of the basic principles of financial and management accounting. The topics covered include accounting statements, profit and loss accounts, cost analysis, and budget planning and control.

The Finance Manual for Non-Financial Managers: The Power to Make Confident Financial Decisions
Paul McKoen, Leo Gough
Harlow: Financial Times Prentice Hall, 1999
319pp (Smarter Solutions Series)
ISBN: 0273644939
The book aims to give the non-financial manager a practical introduction to financial management and control. It explains the basics of accounting and financial reports, with separate chapters covering costing, pricing, project analysis, corporate taxation, financing, and risk management. The accounting implications of acquisitions are also discussed.